LEAVE A LEGACY
THAT COUNTS

LEAVE A LEGACY THAT COUNTS

CREATE ONE AT ANY AGE

Terrie Davoll Hudson

Alpharetta, GA

ISBN: 978-1-63183-600-8 - Paperback
eISBN: 978-1-63183-601-5 - ePub
eISBN: 978-1-63183-602-2 - mobi

Library of Congress Control Number: 2019905148

Printed in the United States of America   0 7 0 6 2 0

⊗This paper meets the requirements of ANSI/NISO Z39.48-1992
(Permanence of Paper)

GET YOUR FREE GIFT!

5 Break-Free Steps for On-Purpose Living

30 Things to Do Intentionally

Intentional Assessment Living Worksheet

Free download at

www.terriehudson.com/legacyleaps

*To Britt and Eden
and all my unborn grandchildren.*

Carve your name on hearts, not tombstones. A legacy is etched into the minds of others and the stories they share about you.

—Shannon Alder

CONTENTS

Acknowledgments

I don't know how I would have gotten up every day to write without the support of Anita Henderson, "The Author's Midwife." Thank you for being my coach and my cheerleader, and for helping me to give birth to my first book.

I appreciate the special people who indulged me and were so gracious during our interviews. I especially enjoyed breaking bread and drinking tea with those in the DFW area. Thank you for your time and candor. Kisses to each of you: Diane Fields Chesley, Joni Arison, Alexis Dennard, Jami Lee Gainey, Debby Feir, and Lorraine Toliver.

A special shout-out goes to beta readers Celena Evans, Janice Brown-Woods, Stephanie Coleman-Smith, and Alexis Dennard. I appreciate your comments and suggestions.

My beloved husband, Elliott, is always supportive and forever patient, even when I have long since talked past his interest level. You make room for me to do what I love, and I love you for it.

Thank you to my tribe. You are always in my corner: daughter Brittany Hudson, sister-in-law Ozella Hailey, brother J. Larry Davoll, and dad James L. Davoll Sr. My life would be so boring and sad without each of you. You bring me such joy. I can always count on you for a mirror, laughs, a night of dancing, and sincere, unconditional love.

To everyone who took the journey of life with me, beginning with my mother. I know she is delighted that I funded this book with legacy money she bequeathed to me. Mu is reading this up in heaven and telling Grandma and Granddaddy all about what their little "Hollywood" has written. Aunt Leola is listening in the heavenly kitchen as she bakes biscuits. Aunt Colon is walking up fast, saying to Mu, "Child, tell the story again." I have no legacy without their love, support, teaching, and examples. Without them, I am nothing.

And to the author and finisher of every word, I thank you, Lord.

INTRODUCTION

I hadn't planned to write this book. It developed out of a keynote speech I delivered at Troy University at their second annual Alabama Leadership Conference. The keynote address was entitled "Making Your Leadership Legacy Count." At the close of the day, several participants reached out to me expressing how impactful my address was. They shared that my personal story was inspirational to them. They wanted to hear more about the subject and about me.

So, this book is the result of that propitious day. I had no idea that my words and my story would impact people in that way. Most people don't know the value of their story, so I suppose I'm no different in that regard. But, what I've realized about the value of story and its impact on one's legacy inspired me to take action.

The direction of my message morphed considerably from the speech to the book. The initial keynote message was from a business or professional perspective. This book is more inclusive and shines light on creating a legacy in all areas of your life. Everyone leaves a legacy, whether they are conscious of it or not. I want you to consciously decide to build your legacy and to make it count.

Most people think of legacy as something left behind after someone—usually a senior citizen—dies. Here, I challenge that presumption in two ways: 1.) Legacy is for the present, as well as for the future; and 2.) legacy is left by people of all ages; it is not something that only the seniors among us can or should develop. So, whether you are male or female, young or old, rich or poor, successful or climbing toward success, now is your time to create and to live a legacy that counts.

It is my sincere desire to prompt you to do four things as you experience your legacy journey:

1. Discover or rediscover your true, full-spectrum why

2. Let go of anything blocking you from achieving your legacy

3. Deliberately establish what your legacy will include

4. Start building your legacy now

When you take these actions, you will undoubtedly create a legacy of which you can be proud. With intentional, daily acts—big and small—you will forge a powerful, sustainable impact on those around you. That amounts to a whole heap of good in the world. You are called to live life, to leave a legacy that counts. You are called to leave a legacy, because mankind is commanded to recognize the needs of others and to respond accordingly. You are beckoned to leave a legacy, because without one your life ends with you. The circle of life is enriched by the gifts that are bestowed upon you and by those you pass on.

I have an unshakeable belief in God. Everything about me is rooted in this belief, which was imparted to me by my family as part of their legacy. As a result, I see the world through my God-centered lens. And who are those relatives who left this legacy for me?

First are my maternal grandparents, Robert and Rosa Spann. They were what you'd call "salt of the earth" kind of folks. Granddaddy and Grandma lived a simple and often hard life in South Carolina. Born in 1900 and 1908, respectively, neither of them put up with nonsense or disruption. I knew they loved me by the actions they took, but I don't remember ever hearing them utter the words "I love you." What I do remember every day of my life are the words they lived by and shared their entire lives: words like, "Your word is your bond," "Lie down with dogs and get up with fleas," and "Every pot (tub) must sit on its own bottom."

Next, and most important in my life, was my mother, Catherine, whom I called Mu (sounds like the "o" in *mother* without the "ther"). She was the fourth child born to Robert and Rosa. My mother was a hell of a woman. She was highly intelligent, always impeccably dressed, stalwart, and had a tender heart. She was brilliant, and struggled with mental illness beginning in her late thirties. She was often shunned by her family members, who didn't understand her condition. None of them wanted to talk about it, which saddened her and our immediate family greatly. Despite that, she created an incredible legacy for my brothers and me, for her community, and for her students. My grandparents' words lived in her, and she passed them down to us as she lived her life. She was such an inspiration that she truly deserves a memoir written for her.

That's another book. Let's get through this one first.

The words of my mother and her parents live not only in me and my siblings; they live in my daughter and are awakening in my granddaughter. And I pass them lovingly on to you throughout this book. It is their legacy, and now it is part of mine.

CHAPTER ONE

WHAT IS LEGACY?

A thing is mighty big when time and distance cannot shrink it.
—Zora Neale Hurston

1

Growing up in walking distance of so many relatives in Columbia, South Carolina, was wonderful for me. I would walk to play with cousins on both sides of my family, and I would visit anytime I wanted to with the only set of living grandparents I had: Robert and Rosa (Green) Spann.

My grandfather died when I was ten years old. He was always sitting on the screened porch reading while my brothers, cousins, and I played out in the side yard. Granddaddy was a stern man, so some of the grandchildren were afraid to talk to him, but I wasn't. One of my favorite interactions with him occurred frequently and always in the same way. I'd open the screen door, enter the screened cinder-block porch, and greet him.

"Hey, Grandaddy. What you doin'?" I'd ask in my bravest voice. Then, I knew what was coming.

"Hey, gal, sit down here." He would point to the old, green, metal swing next to him. That thing always creaked, but I loved sitting in it, perhaps because the other side was typically reserved for Grandma. I was one of the few grandchildren who ever took the time to sit with Granddaddy.

I'd sit on the porch swing beside him. He would hand me his Bible and ask me to read whatever passage was open. I'd read until he told me to stop. "I like it when you read," he would say. "You read with feeling, and you pronounce the words the right way."

That brought about a particular pride inside of me. I was happy that I pleased him and felt especially smart. I remembered that feeling every time I was asked to read in school or when standing up to give big-girl speeches for Easter. Nowadays, I would say that I felt validated and empowered to speak in my own voice.

Sometimes I had an ulterior motive for joining Granddaddy. I'd tell him that all the grandchildren wanted to go to Mr. Charles Henry's store to buy cookies or candy. That meant each of us needed a nickel. He would give me nickels for everyone and slip me a dime. Of course, I pocketed my dime and never told the others about my good fortune. I found out years later from my brother that Granddaddy always gave a little something extra to the kid with the guts to ask.

Now, I recognize the real power of those times with Granddaddy. He demonstrated constantly and perfectly that reading was important to him. Reading the Bible centered him. Those ancient texts reminded him of the legacy he was taught, about how to live a good life, how to treat others, and how to stand up for your beliefs and have self-respect.

Reading the newspaper and other materials kept him up to date on local happenings and gave him a chance to visit foreign lands virtually. We shared that deep love of reading. He was the first person, aside from my mother, who affirmed my love for words and fostered my enjoyment of reading aloud, an activity I enjoy to this very day.

Granddaddy didn't leave me money. The legacy he left for me was so much more. I believe he understood the true meaning of legacy and the impact it could have on others. I am grateful that I learned that from him, and I'm happy to share it here with you.

WHAT IS YOUR LEGACY?

Life is generally thought of as a series of seconds, minutes, hours, days, weeks, months, and years. In reality, life and time are the measure of what you achieve and the impact you have on your family, community, and the world. Those achievements and that impact, in essence, are your legacy. Those minutes, weeks, and years are happening now. That means you are creating your legacy as you live. The legacy you are creating is the impact you will leave for the future.

What impact are you having now? What impact will you have once your time has ended?

Like most people, you probably go about your daily life giving little thought to what you leave behind. What will people remember about you once you have left your job, your community, or this earth? Whether you realize it or not, you are leaving a legacy. You are making an impact on other people, on your environment, on the world by the way you live, by the actions you take, by the words you speak.

Would you rather leave a legacy by default or by design? Undoubtedly, others will decide what they remember about you. But, the power lies in you choosing the legacy you want to leave, and then living that legacy in everything you do. You have that power.

Whatever your circumstances—being poor, young, old, uneducated, living in a foreign land, female, or male—there is no excuse for not creating and leaving a legacy that counts. A legacy that counts must be demonstrated by you and impactful to others while you are alive. It must also last well beyond your departure, whether that is a departure from your current community, your job, your department, or from this world.

So, what is your legacy? What impact are you currently making on others? If you've never considered this, don't worry. You will discover more about your legacy and how to shape it into what you want it to be.

TYPES OF LEGACY

In my study of what legacy is, I have noted a number of areas that can be defined as legacy:

- Financial

- Material

- Biological

- Values

Most people think of legacy as financial—in the form of cash, life-insurance policies, mutual funds, and the like—that is passed on from one generation to the next. This is indeed one form of legacy; however, unless the next generation is instilled with an appreciation of the financial legacy and the knowledge to grow and retain it for future generations, this form of legacy can disappear in as little as one or two generations. Although this legacy counts to those who have a chance to enjoy it, future generations may not have the opportunity to benefit from it.

In my youth, I thought that leaving a legacy meant I had to earn a lot of money (or find a bundle of money somewhere), so I could leave a wad for my children who were going to expect it. I must admit that I admired families that demonstrated this kind of legacy, and I used to wax longingly about the randomness of being born into such a family. I love my parents, but had money been the most important thing to me, I wouldn't have chosen them. Sorry, Mu, Da. (Da is what I call my father.)

Material legacy takes the form of land, homes, jewelry, heirlooms, vintage clothing, artwork, household items, and other possessions that can be left to others as a remembrance of you. These are items you collect, and perhaps use and enjoy, while you are alive, then bequeath to the next generation or donate to charity when you die. Although these items may serve as a memory of you for those who possess them, there is a limit to the broader reach and long-term impact they have. If the item is lost or damaged, so goes your legacy. In this way, material items may not always qualify as a legacy that counts.

The legacy you leave can also be biological in nature. Biological legacies—often referred to as genetics or heredity—can be obvious, and some not so obvious. Everyone tells you that you look like your father. You like that, although you wish you hadn't gotten his big ears. You may have the gorgeous, big, brown eyes that your grandmother had. Or, as in my case, you look at your hands and see your mother's hands. You probably take these genetic likenesses for granted, but they are, in fact, legacy, because they were passed to you.

Congenital anomalies—such as the BRCA1 gene marker linked to breast and ovarian cancer; polydactylism, which presents as extra digits on the hands or feet; or cystic fibrosis—run through families from generation to generation, and can also be viewed as biological legacies. Although biological and genetic traits are indeed legacies, you did nothing to earn them, have no control over receiving them, and do not control or influence their impact on future generations.

And then there is the legacy of values. I believe this is the most meaningful and enduring type of legacy. Values, also known as principles, tenets, and ethics, reflect what you care about most in your life. You may not have considered this, but you already have a set of personal core values. A

list of your core values might include some of the following:

Take a moment to identify your core values. Are you leading your life accordingly? Will you leave a legacy based on your core values? You can, and here's how.

Living according to your values gives you a yardstick by which to measure your actions and decisions. Living according to your values is the North Star that guides you to create a legacy that counts. For instance, if you value community, then you will not rest until you find ways to contribute to your community. If service to others is high on your values list, you will serve others in manners big and small.

During the writing of this book, George H. W. Bush, forty-first president of the United States, died. He served our country with grace and dignity in several major roles—as president, vice president, CIA director, ambassador, and as one of the youngest naval aviators. I was struck by the overwhelming response, including my own, to his passing. I wasn't moved by the accolades of what he accomplished as president, although he had a remarkable four years. What touched me most were the stories of the interactions he had with reporters, White House household staff, his friends, and of course, his family. He left several types of legacies, but the ones that stood out to me were those expressly demonstrating his values:

- Kindness and real caring, even for his political opponents

- Deep love of country

- Unconditional love for his family and friends

There is a prevailing legacy in you, too. Anchoring and living your life according to your values create a long-lasting legacy. A legacy of values can endure forever.

ELEMENTS OF A GOOD LEGACY

You may wonder what makes up a good legacy. Elements of a legacy that count include reputation, actions repeated over time, and character. A good legacy is fueled by your aspirations, attitude, truthfulness, and authenticity. These attributes determine what and how you convey your legacy to others. A respectable reputation and wholesome character are the building blocks of a distinguished legacy.

Regardless of which type of legacy you leave, your legacy can be perceived by others as either negative or positive. While you cannot control how others think, you have the power to influence their perceptions by your actions, your words, and the energy you bring to and leave in any situation.

For example, you could have a million dollars you want to leave to a charity. If at the mention of your name, people think "liar," "swindler," and "crook," your sullied reputation could stop charities from accepting your generous donation. Nonprofit organizations need every dollar they can get, and would hate to refuse your money, but might do so to avoid potentially bad publicity that your reputation could bring. Hence, your good intentions aren't welcomed.

So, good character and a good reputation are foundational elements for a solid legacy. Character is what a person is; reputation is what he is supposed to be. Character is in himself; reputation is in the mind of others.[1]

Since reputation is what others think of you, your reputation may not be who you really are; it could be false or otherwise misinterpreted. It is, however, based on something you have left behind with others. Unfortunately, you don't have absolute control over the opinions people form about you; however, you can form and shift people's thinking of you by your actions. Or, in rare cases, someone decides to test your reputation, and in the process changes their opinion of you.

A simple case in point: My longtime friend, Diane Chesley, worked with a woman who had a reputation for being really mean to everyone in the organization. The coworker—we'll call her Prudence—was so cold and mean that coworkers hated interacting with her. She probably didn't really want to be mean. In fact, Diane suspected that Prudence was hurting in some way. Instead of returning Prudence's unsavory disposition, Diane decided to respond to Prudence in the direct opposite.

"One day, I just hugged her," Diane said. "She pulled back a little, but I wouldn't let her go. I held her closer. After that, she slowly warmed up, and over time, we became friends."

In the days and weeks following, others in the organization noticed with surprise the shift in how Prudence interacted with Diane. They wanted to know how Diane had befriended Prudence.

Diane's reply: "I had simply shown her that I loved her unconditionally."

With a simple hug, Diane's perception of Prudence shifted. She saw Prudence as someone who just needed love and appreciation. Diane decided that she would meet Prudence's negative attitude with kindness. Unfortunately, most of their colleagues were still very skeptical and continued to avoid Prudence. Although Prudence's behavior was changing, her reputation for meanness remained the same in most people's minds; therefore, regardless of whether Prudence might have been creating a legacy of hard work, excellence, or leadership, her reputation was that of meanness.

Your reputation, like your legacy, is built over time. It is reinforced by your previous actions and the stories other have shared about you; therefore, your reputation goes hand in hand with your legacy, and follows you even when your behavior has changed. The one thing, however, that has the power to override a negative reputation is your character.

Although your reputation is important, your character is what matters most. Character is who you are deep inside, not who strangers or acquaintances say you are. Your character is your essential nature, and is formed over time by how you think and conduct yourself. You demonstrate your character by your judgment, decisions, and actions toward others. Think of your character as your virtual business card. You carry it with you and present it every single day.

People make snap conclusions about you based on how you dress, speak, walk, or from a single interaction with you. They do not and cannot truly know you from those superficial attributes, but they think they do. Even so, you shed light on who you are through your character.

The people closest to you have the most insight into who you really are. They know your true character, because they have interacted with you over time and in various situations. They know who and how you are on your good days and on your bad days. In essence, they know your character.

Are you happy with who they believe you to be? Does their perception of you mirror your true character?

Consider this: If you think you are helpful and kind, but everyone most familiar with you—your spouse, children, parents, or close associates—disagrees, then you have a problem. Your true character doesn't match your beliefs about yourself. Consider the opinions of family and close friends as being closer to the truth about your character than what's in your head. You have work to do when those two perspectives of your character don't match.

That is different from having a public persona or reputation that doesn't match your character. This mismatch can have devastating impacts on you and your livelihood.

Look at two journalists to see the distinction clearly. Lester Holt, a journalist and *NBC Nightly News* anchor, has a stellar reputation. He is a fine journalist and reporter. His on-air and off-air behavior appear to be the same. He challenges false statements, and he demonstrates a deep abiding love for his wife and family. He has often been an announcer for the Westminster Kennel Club Dog Show. (You've got to love a black man who loves dogs enough to do that.) Holt's character and his reputation line up positively.

On the other hand, Matt Lauer, formerly of the *Today Show*, was also a good television-news anchor. Fans of the *Today Show* will always remember his educational globetrotting adventures in *Where in the World Is Matt Lauer?* He projected a wholesome guy-next-door persona; however, rumors of his philandering circulated in the tabloid media for years. There were also frequent rumors of marital strife between him and his second wife. Eventually, this all panned out as truth. NBC terminated Lauer following allegations of inappropriate sexual behavior. In Lauer's case, what he presented to viewers and how he really lived did not match. His bad-boy reputation and character did match, but in a negative way; therefore, Lauer's legacy as a stellar journalist has been tainted by his negative reputation, fueled by poor character.

Certainly, your character and reputation accumulate to determine the value of your legacy; therefore, leaving a legacy that counts means using the best of what you have been given to create and multiply goodness for a person, a business, or this planet. Although that may sound simple, it can be hard to do, unless you are aware of the power you have to make it so.

SIZE DOESN'T MATTER

Your legacy may be big or small. Size isn't what matters; what matters is that you look for ways to create sustainable impacts every day. This magnificent planet is full of ingenious people who explore ways of improving life for all.

One of my favorite inventors is the scientist Thomas Alva Edison. Even with all the technological inventions of the last fifty years, none have been more impactful than those made by Edison. Edison once said, "I never perfected an invention that I did not think about in terms of the service it might give others." And boy, did he mean that. People all over the planet enjoy the fruits of his labor every day. Edison gave us the electric lightbulb, electricity generation and distribution systems, sound-recording devices, the motion-picture camera, development of native rubber plants, the talking doll, and numerous contributions to the tel-ecommunications industry. Even the electric cars of today run because of Edison's development of the battery.

Edison died in 1931 and is still one of the most prolific inventors in history, having left a huge body of work that continues to impact the world. He also left a great example of inquisitiveness, steadfastness in the pursuit of ideas and ideals, and hard work.

Some legacies start off small and become huge. Consider the Little Free Libraries that have sprung up across the world. What started out as a small gesture has become a movement that influences immeasurable people. Book lovers are creating fun, cute shelves and boxes in their yards, and filling them with free books to lend. Neighbors are encouraged to take a book to read and to put books back in the library. This is a small gift that can only be measured by the joyous response from people who borrow books and from the camaraderie built from chance en-counters at the Little Free Libraries.

The late Todd Bol, creator of these neighbor-hood lending libraries, was inspired by the micro-library movement in Portland, Oregon. He create-ed a miniature one-room schoolhouse, filled it with books, and posted it on his lawn as a tribute to his late mother. Bol and his partner started building these little libraries and posting them in neighborhoods all across the United States. They then set a goal to register 2,500 lending libraries in neighborhoods and communities. They exceeded that goal by more than three hundred, and inspired a movement where others create their own tiny libraries. Now, more than 75,000 Little Free Library reading outposts can be found in over eighty-eight countries, where neighborhood "librarians" increase access to books for children and adults in their communities. Talk about a small impact growing into a huge one! Bol took a simple way to exchange books and created a global impact.

THE SECRET TO MAKING YOUR LEGACY COUNT

Why is it that some people lead a life of meaning and purpose, and others do not? You see it often even in the same family. Parents smile and speak excitedly about one adult child, yet cringe when they talk about another one. Both children received the same parental guidance and support, early education, and financial stability, yet one excels and the other one falls off the rails. Or, you read of someone who rises out of poverty to achieve great success. Meanwhile, tough neighborhoods and poverty engulf many others who remain seemingly helpless and distraught.

What is the difference that creates such vastly polar results in people? Is it happenstance? Is it where they come from, sheer willpower, or lack of obstacles? Perhaps it is their perspective on luck versus opportunities.

The sole difference between those who create a legacy that counts and those who do not—given the same favorable or unfavorable circumstances—is intention. You'll learn more about the value of intentionality in Chapter 4.

Regardless of your status in life, if you do not consciously intend for your legacy to count, it won't, plain and simple. Yes, you will leave a legacy, but more than likely it won't matter to you, and therefore, it will not matter to others. So, before you start leaning on excuses as to why you can't leave a legacy that counts, let's address some misnomers to see why intention overrides them every time when it comes to your legacy.

HAPPENSTANCE

"Happenstance is a coincidental event. If you call your brother on the phone, that is intentional. If you bump into him in a restaurant, it's happenstance."[2] If you truly want to make an impact, why would you leave it to chance, happenstance, or coincidence? You are more likely to find success with intention than to stumble upon it accident-ally; therefore, leaving a legacy that counts is not something that just happens by coincidence.

BACKGROUND

If you come from a family that has for generations left legacies of money, land, jewels, foundations, and buildings named for them, you have enjoyed the coincidence of being born into that family. Unlike your ancestors, that background (or legacy) of wealth might not become your own personal legacy. Unless you intentionally decide to use your background to contribute to the good of your descendants or to the good of mankind, your background does not factor into you creating a legacy that counts.

WILLPOWER

Linked closely to happenstance, willpower is essentially the opposite of intention. Here, you are hoping, wishing, and forcing yourself—mentally and emotionally—to pursue or resist something. That is not how great legacies are created. When you are clear, focused, passionate, committed, and intentional about leaving a legacy that counts, willpower is not needed.

OBSTACLES

I read *The Rainbow Comes and Goes* by Anderson Cooper and his mother Gloria Vanderbilt, primarily because I really liked the title. As it suggests, life is full of unbelievably good experiences, successes, and great joy. It is also full of despair, sadness, fear, and seemingly insurmountable hurdles. Jumping over those hurdles and obstacles can be difficult. It takes courage and skill to make the leap successfully.

There are a host of stories about people who faced unthinkable challenges and came back from disaster. None are more breathtaking than Aron Ralston's story. In 2003, Ralston was hiking alone in a canyon in Utah. On his descent, a boulder dislodged and fell on his right arm, crushing and trapping his right hand. He tried everything to free his arm, but couldn't. He had a couple day's supply of food and water. When that ran out, he drank his own urine to survive. Ralston prepared to die, but never gave up. With no circulation, his arm began to decompose. He decided to do the unthinkable. Using his pocket knife, he cut off his arm. Ralston later had to rappel down the sixty-five-foot wall one-handed, and then walk out of the canyon. Today, Ralston still hikes and climbs mountains. He is a riveting motivational speaker who says he did not lose his hand, but gained his life back.

There are no obstacles big enough to keep you from leaving whatever legacy is in your heart when you have the intention to do so. Obstacles are bumps and stumps in the road that you have to get around. Your internal fortitude is strengthened when you're confronted with challenges that seem too hard to overcome. With intention, you can bear down and stay committed to working through them, and in time, you will.

LUCK

When someone says they never get a fair shake in life or do not have good luck, they are overlooking the chance to seize opportunities. Relying on luck or waiting for others to provide a hand up does not demonstrate the actions of someone with the intention to leave a legacy that counts. I'm reminded of the shade tree university in my old neighborhood.

My friends and I used to skip through our neighborhood in the warm months of the 1960s. We would pass a grove of huge pine trees where black men, after or without work, would play checkers, drink beer, and talk trash to each other. My mother called it "shade tree university." She said there was more knowledge and potential under the trees than you could imagine. The men had no college degrees. Some hadn't graduated from high school. But, they shared what they knew among themselves and anyone else who would listen. Collectively, the men could talk on just about any subject.

Those were difficult times for black people, especially for black men, so they didn't see beyond their circumstances. They didn't see (or seize) the opportunities my mother saw for herself and for her children. Those men had so much to give, but were met with roadblocks that appeared as bad luck, causing them to miss out on opportunities to build an incredible legacy for themselves and potentially for others. Who knows what they could have contributed if they had set the intention to leave a legacy that counts?

Good or bad luck is all up to chance. Of course, take advantage of good luck when it comes, but don't use bad luck as a crutch. Opportunities reveal themselves every day. Train yourself to be aware of them. Be in tune to what is happening around you at work, in your community, in the media, and in your neighborhood schools. Genuinely look at people and their circumstances. What do you see that makes you well up inside with anger, pride, disgust, excitement? Those feelings are good indicators of where opportunities lie for you to make a difference. Those areas can inspire you to intentionally find more meaning personally while making contributions and creating your legacy.

LEGACY LEAPS

- Decide on the type of legacy you want to develop. Is it primarily financial? Material? One of values? There is no right or wrong answer. Just be honest with yourself and be authentic.

- What values do you carry forward from your parents and grandparents?

- Which values do you want to keep and grow, and which ones should you drop now?

- Do your actions, character, and reputation synthesize into the legacy you are creating?

- In what ways are you being intentional with creating your legacy that counts?

CHAPTER TWO

KNOW YOUR *WHY*

The soul which has no fixed purpose in life is lost; to be everywhere, is to be nowhere.
—Michel de Montaigne

Cleaning out my home-desk files a few months after I retired was a bigger job than I'd expected. I had squirreled away all manner of personal documents and resources. There were training packages I'd developed, notes from where I'd taught myself to become highly proficient in digital spreadsheets, presentations on mentoring, coaching assessments, and so much more. You name it, I probably had it—and most of it needed to go.

In the midst of all the professional downsizing, I came across an interesting file. It included the results of several personality tests and 360-degree feedback assessments I had taken over the years. I spread them all out on the floor of my office anticipating pretty much the same story from each of them. To my delight, I could clearly see growth in specific important areas, such as listening better, being more accessible, and managing conflicts. Several areas that I'd deliberately worked on improving became leadership strengths for me. The common thread and constant outcome in all of these instruments spoke to my *why*.

"Excellent in building skills in others, results oriented, sees possibilities and potential in things and people, leads in an organized way, doesn't like to waste her time, can be impatient, tough-minded with a caring heart." Those comments were listed on one assessment. Reading them swelled my pride in a career at which I had worked hard and given my all. All of this makes sense to me in the context of my *why*.

I have known for a few decades that my purpose in life is to uplift people, to coach them to challenge their self-perceptions, and to help them move forward. Part of my purpose is to ask, "Why not?" I fulfill this calling in every aspect of my life, be it at home, at church, at work, or in social settings. This challenging question has become part of my legacy. Those who get to know me well will undoubtedly, at some point in our relationship, hear me ask them the question "Why not?" As simple as it sounds, this question has the power to challenge others to remove the fear and excuses, and to do the very thing they desire.

You want to move to the next level in your career, but you haven't done the research to uncover the requirements? I ask, "Why not?"

You want to pack up your family, move to a new city, and live the life of your dreams? I ask, "Why not?"

You want to give up your six-figure job and become a hot-yoga instructor in Costa Rica? I ask, "Why not?"

You want to obtain your undergraduate degree, but you're over fifty years old? I ask, "Why not?"

You want to start a new ministry, but you've never done that before? I ask, "Why not?"

Asking "Why not?" helps you get to your true *why*. Answering the question empowers you to shift your thinking and brings into focus your real desires. Asking "Why not?" forces you to let go of entrenched ideas and assumptions, and replace them with new ideas that provoke and inspire you.

What does it mean to know your *why*, and why is that even important? Knowing your *why* means understanding your deep purpose for doing what you say you want to do. I'm not talking about the surface reason you give people; I'm talking about the honest-to-goodness driving force behind your goals, dreams, and desires. This is a foundational principle of leaving a legacy that counts.

Being clear about the legacy you want to leave, and why you want to leave that specific legacy, will guide your every action, decision, and behavior. Clarity is the key to getting from here to there on your pathway to leaving a legacy that counts. And, the process to get clear about your *why* involves asking yourself some tough questions . . . and answering them.

You are here for a reason. Each person has a path full of myriad experiences. All culminate in the creation of the true person. Not a single person on the planet can replace or usurp your mission. You must determine your *why* to be truly fulfilled.

You can find it, but only by looking fervently inside yourself. Living can seem hard sometimes, but deciding to live the life you're destined to live makes your life fuller and richer.

Even the detours in your life are relevant to you becoming your full self. Detours are paths and actions you take when you aren't ready to take on the mantle of your purpose. Those sidesteps prepare you to do what you are called to do.

Remember those personality tests and assessments I poured over as I transitioned from my corporate career? Each one gave me great insight into myself. There are dozens of psychological tests available to reveal, through scientific and psychological methodology, the way you view yourself and the world. They assess the way you process information, make decisions, how you relate to others, and highlight the values which matter most to you. Although you don't need to take a personality test to learn these things about yourself, the tests are structured to provide valuable insights into yourself that might take you decades to discover. But, finding your *why* is different and takes more than external testing.

Finding your *why* is not really about you at all. It's how your spiritual being connects to others. It's what you were designed to do here on Earth. Learning as much as you can about your true self can help you be your best self. You arrive at your true self when you are aware of your purpose and are in touch with your feelings. Being connected to your purpose and feelings allows you to experience your best life. Experiencing your best life leads you to become the best you possible.

What Fulfills You?

If you don't know who you are, you cannot be fulfilled, and you most likely will struggle to find your *why*. You may spend far too much time looking at others and trying to see yourself in them. You follow others because they look like they have it together, or they are living a life you think is exciting. None of this helps you, because you must first know yourself. Looking for others to define you is unproductive and can be destructive. Becoming a carbon copy of someone else is a detour from the path that is yours.

Today's social media has skewed everyone's perspective of what real life looks like. People post photos of themselves that have been edited and filtered so much that you don't know what they really look like. They post only the fabulous segments of their lives. You follow people who you have never met, and you know only the sanitized version they present of themselves. You believe their lives are more fulfilling and on point than your own. But, their lives are just like yours. Oh, sure, they may have more money, wear designer clothes, or vacation on islands you may never visit, but underneath all the glitz and glamour, they share some of the same life experiences that you do. Your life is—or will be—full of trials, bumps, scuffs, successes, and losses. And so are theirs, because that's what life is all about.

It is also easy to focus on material things. The world tells you that your worth is determined by what you own. You are led to believe that if you have nothing, then you are nothing. So, you seek stuff as an outward presentation of what you want others to perceive about you. You buy expensive cars, houses, vacations, clothes, and body enhancements, yet you are still unfulfilled.

The thirteenth-century Persian poet Rumi summed it up perfectly when he said, "Maybe you are searching among the branches for what only appears in the roots." Is Rumi speaking of you? Do you look at everything and everyone around you to define what is important to you? I hope not, because what others do, what others have, and what they experience has no impact on your personal fulfillment. Fulfillment happens on the inside, from the inside. Your fulfillment guides you to understand your *why*.

HAPPY VS. CONTENT

So often, people are driven by how happy something or someone makes them feel. You do not need to know your *why* to be happy. Happiness is a momentary emotion caused by immediate gratification or results. When you get the job, you are happy. When the apple of your eye finally says, "I love you," you are happy.

When you win a prize, achieve a goal, complete a task, or experience a desire, you are happy.

However, contentment—being at ease with your circumstances while working to improve them—is a result of knowing your *why*. Knowing your purpose—your *why*—increases your level of true contentment and opens you up for realizing your legacy. Contentment allows you to reach a state of mind where you are satisfied, fulfilled, and gratified with yourself.

You need not be happy continuously to be content with yourself and your life. A simple example of the difference: You may be unhappy that you didn't win the marathon race while being very satisfied (content) with how you prepared for it and how you ran it.

I learned the difference between happiness and contentment during my marriage. My husband, Elliott, and I celebrated our fifteenth wedding anniversary in 2000. We had just come through a rough patch in our marriage and were a stronger couple than ever. I was happy, and so was he. When we first married, I made him promise that he and I would grow old together, that we would buy two big rocking chairs and sit side by side holding hands, looking at beautiful sunsets when we got old. None of us is promised old age, but we still made that promise to each other. Years later, that promise was tested beyond anything I could have imagined.

In January 2001, Elliott had a back pain that didn't go away. He thought it was the result of lifting and moving a large home freezer. He went to see his doctor, who found nothing, and suggested that Elliott get a colonoscopy as part of his annual checkup. Then, our world imploded. That routine colonoscopy showed that Elliott had stage IV colon cancer. He was given just a few months to live. Through many traumatic months dealing with doctors, hospitals, and insurance carriers, I fought like a warrior to get him into a new trial, a variety of surgeries, and the best care available.

Throughout those grueling months watching my husband suffer pain and discomfort—and as I experienced my Cinderella life seemingly slip away—I cried my eyes out, washed my face, made it up again, put on my best outfit, and smiled countless times before going to visit him in the hospital. I never wanted him to see my sorrow or my fear. I never wanted him to know how scared I was that he wouldn't be able to keep his promise to me. I wanted him to know that I still believed we would sit on that porch in our rocking chairs and watch the sunset.

Eighteen years later, I am still Elliott's primary health advocate. Yes, he survived and is still living fairly well. Over the years, we have shared many sunsets (although we haven't purchased those rocking chairs yet). Those have been some of the happiest moments I've experienced. Along the way, however, I learned to be content being the primary breadwinner for our family. I have learned to be content attending social events alone, because Elliott oftentimes doesn't have the energy to accompany me. Contentment became joy when I realized that God has equipped me to be whatever my husband needed me to be. God has equipped me to lead a fulfilling life of my own.

I smile a lot these days. My smiles truly come from a place of contentment and not necessarily happiness. This isn't to diminish the importance of contentment. There is joy in contentment. Oftentimes, contentment is a comforting friend on the journey to happiness. Knowing and living in your *why* can give you unbelievable contentment. You may not be happy with experiences or responsibilities in your life, but when you know your *why*, you can be content, find happiness in other experiences, and live your legacy.

YOUR *WHY* IS NOT YOUR REASON

When interviewing candidates to work for me, I often asked why they wanted the job. Most gave some lofty or insincere responses that they thought sounded good, such as "I want to add value to the company," or "I want be part of a team." When asked what value they would bring that fills a gap in the company, there would be crickets. They had no thoughts or real answers.

Other candidates gave reasons for wanting the job, and frankly, I respected them for their candor. Their responses sounded like, "I need money to pay my bills," "My kid needs health care," and "I need a job I can do well that has great benefits."

Once every few years, someone would answer based on their *why*. When they did, I would sit up straight to listen. One interviewee, I'll call her Sarah, stated, "I want to build peace, and looking at the conflict in the team, I believe I can be a bridge to consensus." After that response—and her response to other thought-provoking questions—I knew that Sarah had researched the organization well enough to identify its struggles, and she clearly saw how to be impactful operating from her *why*.

While several excellent candidates were on my final slate for consideration, I told my boss that I had selected Sarah because she saw a way to use her *why* in the role. He didn't quite understand my enthusiasm for Sarah, and probably thought I'd made a mistake. As it turned out, hiring Sarah became one of the best personnel decisions I had ever made. Although she lacked some of the more technical aspects of the job, Sarah added huge value in negotiating resolutions to difficult client issues.

The difference between your reason and your *why* is as different as Sarah's reason for wanting the job and her *why* for stepping into the position. Sarah's reason could have included many of the reasons the other candidates had stated. After all, she, too, had a family and responsibilities; however, her *why* for wanting to be in that specific position was to solve a challenge she felt uniquely suited to solve. She knew that her natural and developed skills and gifts could be applied to improve the team as a whole, as well as to enhance her own life.

Can you see through Sarah's example that your *why* is bigger than you? Knowing your *why* is knowing exactly what you are here on Earth to do. Your *why* is your purpose. Knowing your purpose gives you hope. Knowing who you are is central to feeling whole and fulfilled.

Operate within your *why* to magnify your gifts and talents. They, and you, will continue to grow throughout your life.

I was watching television a few years ago and heard a story that demonstrates exactly what I mean here. I don't remember the woman's name, so I'll call her Julie, but I remember her story. Julie said that as a child, she enjoyed creating hairstyles on dolls and knew that becoming a hair stylist was the perfect job for her. It would allow her the freedom to own a business, create her own hours, and make a very good living. She thought of this as her calling. Many years later, she had an epiphany that changed her life. Julie discovered that doing hair wasn't her calling at all, but it allowed her to fulfill her purpose as an evangelist. She began serving homeless men and women on the street by cutting their hair, shaving them, and telling them about the good news of Jesus. I remember her chuckling about how her paid clientele and finances grew the more she followed her purpose—her *why*.

So, imagine the most outrageous legacy you could endow your family. Then, get on with using your gifts and talents to build that vision. You are equipped for your journey. Be prepared for the challenges, the joys, and the contentment of a life fully lived.

LEGACY LEAPS

- If you know your *why*—your purpose—write it in a simple statement.

- If you're not sure, write one or two things that you believe are part of your purpose.

- How well are you living, working, and operating within your *why*?

- What actions or behaviors do you take regularly that align with your *why*?

CHAPTER THREE

WHAT'S HOLDING YOU BACK?

Do the thing we fear, and death of fear is certain.
—Ralph Waldo Emerson

Many years ago, I wrote in my journal that I would become a professional inspirational speaker, helping others to become their best selves. I also jotted down a number of book titles that year for books I wanted to write.

I did not do either of those things then. I was afraid to leave my cushy, comfortable job that came with a great salary, a 401K, stock options, and excellent health benefits. So, instead of boldly walking away from my career to realize my dreams, I tried to satisfy bits of them in the roles I chose at work and in my community activism. This worked to a point, but I wasn't wholly gratified.

I was always happy when speaking on leadership and self-improvement topics. I loved getting the feedback that I had inspired those in the audience. But, in reality, I wasn't doing what I was inspiring others to do. I didn't go whole-hog into my ambition. I inched into it until I couldn't avoid taking the leap. I wish I had not waited so long.

What's holding you back from being who you are destined to be? What is keeping you from living and leaving a legacy that counts? For most people, these four primary reasons are the culprits that keep your legacy bound:

1. Fear of failure

2. Feeling unworthy

3. Believing your experiences don't amount to much

4. Lacking a role model

Let's look at each more in depth.

FEAR OF FAILURE

Fear keeps you stuck where you are. You can walk into a room and feel the fear—yours or someone else's. It is palpable. You can smell fear, too. In classrooms, students are afraid instructors might call on them. In staff meetings, employees are afraid to state their opinions or quote facts that are needed to make decisions. When you have these basic fears, you don't step up to do simple things, let alone remarkable things. In reality, you're afraid to fail with an audience looking on. You imagine that failure is final, when in fact failure is learning what not to do when you try it again.

Like many, you could be on the pathway to success, but instead you hide your dreams and goals because you're afraid you'll disappoint your family or friends. You're afraid you will bomb and botch your idea. So, you don't even try.

You might also be fearful of success. If you are successful, you set higher expectations for yourself, then panic at the thought of what might happen should you fail as you climb higher.

You might be surprised to learn that even the "successful" among us fear failure. Adele, the British singer-songwriter, is known for having a beautiful, booming voice. Her song "Someone Like You" is the second-most downloaded song of 2011 in the United Kingdom, according to the Official UK Top 40 Chart. Adele has been very forthright about her almost crippling stage fright, stating publicly that her fear has become worse, not better, the more successful she has become.[3] It has been so bad that she has projectile vomited before going onstage.[4] Adele battles her fear before every live performance, but she goes onstage anyway. Why does she do it? Because writing and singing heartfelt songs that impact others is her *why*.

Don't let fear keep you stuck where you are. Generally, it isn't the big fears, like losing your job, that loom over you. It's the overwhelming anxiety or horror that you will fail if you step out to pursue what's in your heart that holds you back.

If you are among the estimated 73 percent of people who experience glossophobia,[5] you have a fear of speaking in public. Speaking to audiences exhilarates me, so I am fascinated at what scares people about public speaking. Of those I've surveyed, most people list these three public-speaking fears:

1. Lack of confidence. Also related to stage fright, lack of confidence can become so crippling that some people literally lose their voice at the thought of having to speak in public.

2. Unreceptive audience. Many fearful would-be speakers believe that what they have to say may not be well received by their audience, so they clam up, whether in meetings or onstage. They aren't comfortable sharing ideas, because they fear others might think less of them.

3. Perceived poor speaking ability. Some people fear that they are just not good speakers. They compare themselves to more successful speakers, and feel they don't measure up.

These responses and overall aversion to speaking publicly equate to "I am afraid to fail." If you can relate, you may be so afraid of failing that you choose to stifle your ideas, deprive yourself of developing a marketable skill, and allow others to make you feel inferior. The impact of this anxiety, doubt, and fear is bigger than just not speaking out. It shows up in other parts of your life, as well.

Fear of failing in anything in front of peers, family, and friends is daunting. Millions of people are afraid to give voice to their goals because they are afraid of failing. Being afraid of falling flat or disappointing someone should not stop you from pursuing your wildest dreams. Think about all the opportunities that require you to face the possibility of failure in order to succeed. Overcoming this one obstacle will change your life!

I learned that courage is not the absence of fear, but the triumph over it. The brave man is not he who does not feel afraid, but he who conquers that fear.
—Nelson Mandela

So, what legacy do you want to create but haven't had the courage to tell someone about or to make it happen, merely because you're afraid to fail?

Managing fear is a process. There are simple steps you can take to relieve yourself of the burden of fear so you can get on with creating your legacy. Here are six actions to begin managing your fear:

1. **Commit to eliminating the fear.** The rest of the process is straightforward, but you've got to put in the work to achieve the results you want. When you're ready to fight your fear, commit and get to work.

2. **Acknowledge the fear.** It's powerful and

real to you. Rather than masking your fear, admit to being afraid so you can do something about it. So, call it out and confront it.

3. **Drill down.** Explore what really scares you about the situation. Analyze your fear. You can't conquer what you don't fully understand. So, spend time truly understanding the elements that scare you. You have to dissect your fear to determine how to contain it.

4. **Identify where and how the fear manifests itself physically and mentally.** For example, do your palms get sweaty? Does your head hurt when you're in fearful situations? Do you suddenly stutter or have a difficult time putting your thoughts in order? Specifically, how does fear show up in your mind and body?

5. **How does it affect you?** Once you can clearly articulate what the fear is and how it impacts you, you're ready to work on slaying it. Start by making small steps.

6. **How do you cope now?** Reducing stress and anxiety related to fearful situations is helpful. You can use visualization or breathing techniques to calm yourself. Try positive self-talk to redirect your thoughts. Explore a number of coping mechanisms to help you overcome or manage your fear.

Everyone is afraid of something. It's human nature to be frightened of situations that are foreign to you. It's common to be afraid even when you're walking in your purpose, like Adele. Confront fears that keep you bound. You can conquer most fears with a plan and hard work. If you can't conquer them, you can surely find coping mechanisms that allow you to move forward.

FEELING UNWORTHY

Unworthiness. The word itself makes you pause. Who among us is worthy of anything? On occasion, everyone thinks they may not deserve some goodness or accolades that come to them. That is not what I'm talking about here. This feeling of unworthiness runs deep and threatens to pervade your every action. It manifests itself in how you perceive your place in society. Underneath it all is a feeling that your life matters little to you or to others. How, then, can you create and leave a legacy that counts?

Questions and statements of merit that swirl in your brain might sound like this:

- "Who am I? I have nothing of value to share with others."

- "I come from nothing. Who wants to hear from me?"

- "I am not perfect. What will others think of me?"

- "I am not the same caliber of person as he or she."

- "I have only a few followers on social media."

You may occasionally be haunted by thoughts of unworthiness, causing you to have low expectations for just about everything. Perchance you have had difficulties, and you believe you are destined for a hard life. Maybe you have committed some shameful act and believe you deserve self-condemnation, although you have made amends.

Subconscious self-reproach can be subtle. You may feel undeserving of recognition, so you hide yourself, physically and figuratively. Are you the person who studies and prepares hard for a meeting with colleagues, then sits in the back of the room contributing nothing because you don't believe you deserve attention? You tell yourself that you are not smart or worthy enough to go after that job you want. You are not equipped to give anything of value to others.

Stop the negative self-talk. You define your worthiness. Only you prescribe, describe, and determine your worth. Being worthy does not mean that you are perfect, virtuous, or blameless for behavior or actions you may have taken in the past. It means that you are decent and valuable, and that you want to lead a respectable life now.

Where you have been, what you have done, and any characteristics you view as shortcomings do not define your future.

Maya Angelou was a well-known, respected poet, memoirist, singer, actress, and civil rights activist. She left the world with some notable books and poems, like *I Know Why the Caged Bird Sings*, *And Still I Rise*, and "On the Pulse of Morning," which she read at President Bill Clinton's 1993 inauguration.

Angelou's early life was tragic and certainly not a predictor of the acclaimed writer she would become. In her biographical works, Angelou tells of how she was raped at age eight and didn't utter a word for almost five years afterward. During her late teens and early adult years, she was a prostitute, a cook, and the first black female cable-car conductor in San Francisco. Many of Angelou's early experiences would have brought some women to their knees, but not her. She discovered her gifts and talents, and used them without caution. Angelou's words and life are a remarkable inspiration. Through her, we see tragedy, self-love, and love of all humanity. We hear laughter and hope. Angelou inspires us to take the bitter with the sweet to live an incredibly full and rewarding life. That is her legacy.

Overcome your feelings of unworthiness by challenging your beliefs about yourself. You may not look like the people you consider to be more worthy than you. You may not sound like them. You don't have what they have. You don't run in the same circles. You didn't go to the best schools like they did. Believe me when I tell you, none of that matters.

You are worthy because you are "fearfully and wonderfully" created. The fact that you exist affirms that you are worthy. You are just as important as the next person. You have a voice. You have a unique story to tell. Your story has a place on the legacy wheel. The question is not whether you deserve a place in the world, but rather whether the world deserves to hear from you. Your life experiences, dreams, and goals are more important than you can imagine.

Put aside the nagging elf sitting on your shoulder, telling you that you have nothing of value to offer anyone. Do not let self-doubt rob you of becoming who you are destined to be. Do not let it silence you. You are worthy, and you are enough.

Getting to that new place of understanding your worth can be hard. You must work through years of self-doubt and tear down years of believing that you aren't good enough. But, rest assured—you are enough!

Reset your thinking right now. If you must, fake it 'til you make it. Act as if you are enough until you absolutely believe it.

BELIEVING YOUR EXPERIENCES DON'T AMOUNT TO MUCH

Another nagging doubt keeping you from developing your legacy is believing that your experiences and contributions are irrelevant, believing that they mean nothing to anyone else. You may feel unappreciated for what you bring to the table. Or, you feel no accountability for sharing what you've learned, and believe that no one else does, either. Or, perhaps you simply feel that no one cares as much as you do about the things that matter to you.

No experience is merely good or bad. Each one is relevant, for they come together to create the totality of your life. Your life is significant; therefore, so are your experiences. Learn from and appreciate how those experiences shape your thinking and decisions. Claim your experiences. Use them creatively to share your story with others and to help determine your legacy.

As Dr. Martin Luther King Jr. said, "You don't have to see the whole staircase, just take the first step." You have no idea what's in store for you. You merely have to keep moving forward. Again, we are interconnected beings, so you are important to the whole. You must do your part, because someone is depending on you to complete it. Your contributions are absolutely needed, no matter how small or insignificant they might seem at first. Sometimes, even your mistakes can become the solution to someone else's problem.

If you work in an office, you probably use sticky notes from time to time. They have got to be one of the most useful and proliferate office items found around the world. Dr. Spencer Silver, a chemist working for the 3M company, did not set out to create the sticky note. In fact, he was trying to invent the opposite of the low-tack sticky adhesive on the notes you enjoy.[6] Voila! Through his tests, trials, and mistakes to create a different product of use, the sticky note was born. Dr. Silver could not have imagined that the resulting product would become a standard item on almost every desk around the world. Since few people were even aware of his work, not many cared about his efforts at the time. But, look at the success his accidental invention has returned. Can you imagine accidentally creating a legacy of equal value to the world? What an awe-inspiring "mistake" to make!

Here are a couple of lessons to take away from Dr. Silver's experience that might lead you to capitalize on "mistakes" in your life:

1. **Obstacles are a normal part of life.** You begin a project that you've planned out, with well-defined expected results. In the midst of execution, what looks like an obstacle occurs. Time to make some choices. You could give up and abandon the project, or you could do as Dr. Silver did: Stop and examine the stumbling block. Is it useful for other possible applications? Other people? Examine the challenge from a different per-

spective. You may have stumbled upon the answer to a question that has not yet been asked. You may not be in a position to make big discoveries that will change the world, but each discovery you make about yourself or the world around you is important. All your experiences, passions, and abilities combine to shape your legacy.

2. **Go with the flow.** This is a common phrase that generally means to conform or accept situations as they arise. If this seems challenging for you because you like having control and driving toward specific results, take a step back. Learn to let go. Don't try to control or alter everything that doesn't go as you anticipated. Sometimes, it is in your best interest to let situations unfold, and then evaluate the outcomes for their usefulness. At times, you can be so focused on what you want to occur that you miss something equally or more significant during the process. Discern when to evaluate incidents that appear to be off track rather than ignore them. They may not be what they seem. Continue pursuing them if at each step they prove fruitful for you—just not as you'd expected. Letting go of your predetermined ideas and allowing things to happen organically may be just what you need to discover your legacy.

Every experience you have is part of the composition of your life and is an ingredient of your legacy. Oftentimes, these experiences seem random and unimportant. But, as you journey on with the intent to live your best life, the most mundane, frustrating, or seemingly irrelevant incidents come into full view as stepping stones to your legacy.

For example, like every new college graduate, Hoda Kotb expected to find a job right out of college. How hard could it be to get hired as a television reporter? She had a rude awakening when it didn't happen on her first interview. In fact, she went on countless interviews all over the southern United States and was rejected over and over.

Frustrated and disappointed after an unfruitful interview in Florida, she began making her way back home to Virginia. She decided that being a television reporter was not in the cards for her. During the drive, she got lost. On the roadside, she studied her map. (This was back in the day when people used paper maps.) Kotb looked up and saw a billboard for a local CBS TV station. Feeling defeated and having nothing to lose, she drove to the station and asked for an interview. And just like that, she was hired as a reporter.

Just as she was ready to give up and pursue a different career, the job that would launch her career in television appeared. Getting lost turned out to be the best thing that ever happened to her. She didn't see the whole staircase, but she kept walking up the stairs.

In 2018, Hoda Kotb became coanchor of the *Today Show*, where she influences millions of morning-news watchers every day. The universe conspires with you when you let go and flow with situations, especially those in which you have no control. Learn to relax, even when things seem maddening, hard, or disappointing. You will have less stress and strain on your body and your mind. Learn to embrace all your experiences.

Your experiences are unlike those of anyone else. No one else in the universe has encountered the exact set of incidents that you have, nor learned from them what you've learned. All of this blends with your passions, aptitude, and talents to create the crowning glory that is you. Everything you experience is significant. You have a relevant legacy story to create and share. Cherish your experiences and use them to build a legacy that counts.

LACKING A ROLE MODEL

You look around your life and see that everyone is heads down, living day to day. The people you encounter are focused on the most fundamental levels of Maslow's hierarchy of needs: food, water, shelter, financial or personal security. Self-actualization and the pursuit of higher dimensions of life may be off their radar for now.

So, you know of no one who is intentionally thinking about their legacy; therefore, you don't, either. You question the need for putting energy into this process, because no one else is doing so in your life. Well, you may have to lead the way and become a role model for others. This goes back to the importance of knowing your purpose. Use your *why* to create the vision for others to mimic.

> *It is always through those who are unafraid to be different that advance comes to human society.*
> —Raymond B. Fosdick

Joni Arison, one of my favorite bosses, told me an uplifting story about her mother and the women in her community. During the 1950s and '60s, most middle-class American women did not work outside the home. If they did, it was only until they began having children. Once the little ones were born, the women felt that their working days were over.

Joni's mother, Louise Cavallero, decided that she was not going to lead that kind of life. Mrs. Cavallero had no role model, but knew that working and creating a life separate from her husband and children was right for her. So, after the birth of her three children, she returned to the workforce, beginning a long career with the telephone company in Connecticut. She not only worked a job, but aspired to manage people, and achieved the promotions to do so. As long as Joni could remember, both her parents had always worked, so having a working mother was no big deal to her.

When Mrs. Cavallero passed way, Joni and her siblings heard stories of how remarkable their mother had been for her generation. She had returned to work after starting her family, much to the initial chagrin of her friends and neighbors. At the time, they wondered what Louise was doing. Why was an Italian-Catholic married woman not satisfied to stay home cooking, cleaning, and caring for her family?

At the memorial service, several women shared stories of how much they and other women in the community had admired Mrs. Cavallero. They spoke about following her example for years. Mrs. Cavallero inspired them to return to work after their children were born. When she pushed to become a manager at work, other women were encouraged and followed in her footsteps. They credit Mrs. Cavallero for inspiring them to find personal fulfillment outside their homes.

Joni followed in her mother's footsteps and began an illustrious career. When Joni was promoted to management, her boss called Mrs. Cavallero to tell her what an awesome employee Joni was and to share his excitement about her promotion. When he asked Mrs. Cavallero if she knew how talented her daughter was, she said, "Of course, I do. Where do you think she got it from? I wouldn't expect anything less." Today, Joni continues setting a high bar for women as a much-admired officer and leader at her company.

Sometimes people, like Mrs. Cavallero, create the path for others to follow. Other times, it seems role models are more difficult to find; however, if you look for them, you will find them, sometimes in the most unlikely people.

As a director of a call center, I interviewed and hired numerous sales representatives to sell advertising by telephone. Most of them had solid sales skills, and we taught them all they needed to know about our advertising products. One rep was struggling to put it all together successfully and asked a peer for advice. The peer shared his secret to success: "I ear hustle," meaning he eavesdropped on other sales colleagues. He shared how he identified the rep with the best informative sales pitch, listened to how he talked to customers, and learned from him. Then, he adapted everything to fit his personality.

That's what you can do.

If there are no role models in your immediate family or circle of friends, look elsewhere for someone who is creating the life you want. Find someone who is obviously creating a legacy at work, in the community, or even someone on the world stage. Break down what they do and how it can work for you. You can "ear hustle" in lots of ways. Here are a few:

- Read books and articles by or about the person you admire, but can't get up close and personal to learn from firsthand.

- Ask a mentor to introduce you to someone in their network who is doing what you want to do. Be prepared to show your mentor how serious you are about this introduction. Know exactly why the contact is perfect for you. Know what you want to learn and perhaps what you can offer, too.

- Attend local conferences that have speakers whose topics fit with where you'd like to take your next steps.

- Join an organization that allows you to use the skills and talents that come naturally to you. You are sure to find likeminded people and increase your opportunity to learn from them.

It takes work to transform yourself into a legacy creator. There will be things along the journey that threaten to hold you back, but you must not give in to defeat. View these blockages as nothing more than distractions or opportunities to learn and grow.

None of this is easy, but it is worth it. You will be stronger if you persist. You will create your legacy and make it count. Ultimately, you will be more satisfied with yourself.

LEGACY LEAPS

- No fear should discourage you. Confront fears that keep you bound. Write down the dreams that you have not given voice to out of fear. Then,

  o Write down your initial trepidation. Ask yourself, "What's the worst that could happen?"

  o Use the steps in this chapter to begin conquering the most important ones.

  o Repeat until you've mastered them enough to move past them.

- Worthiness is in the heart of the person, not in the eye of the beholder. Your self-talk, as well as circumstances and comments from others, may make you question your worthiness. Stop! Train yourself to create and run a new tape in your mind to combat your own negativity. If you generally exaggerate the negative aspects of situations, try this exercise over the next two weeks:

  o For every negative thought you have, identify two to three positive ones. Write down the positive thoughts and review them at the end of the day. You will have a long list of positive thoughts to reaffirm for yourself in the future.

- o Update your self-talk. Replace "I failed at _____, so I'm a failure" with "I learned how not to do _____. I will regroup and try again."

- Role models and positive people abound. Find others who speak to your heart and mission, and surround yourself with them.

  - o Select two role models. Engage with them personally, if you can.

  - o Seek out local people who are on a similar path as the one you want to walk. See who in your circle knows them, and ask for an introduction. If no introduction is possible, prepare to reach out to them directly.

  - o If you can't find a local inspiration, look elsewhere. Read about global figures, study their habits, and ear hustle to learn from them. Adopt what makes sense for your life.

  - o Do what you must to connect and build several mentoring relationships that are mutually beneficial. And don't be surprised if, down the road, someone starts to see you as their role model!

CHAPTER FOUR

THE POWER OF BEING INTENTIONAL

*Intentional living is the art of making our own choices
before others' choices make us.*
—Richie Norton

There is unmistakable power in being intentional about the things that matter to you. Without intention, you drift aimlessly through life without purpose. Of course, intention requires follow through to be most impactful, but you have to start with a goal. When you have a goal for the legacy you want to leave, and you go about it with intention, you will see so much in your life change for the better. Let me share a story about a woman who has built her life around purposeful living.

Jami Lee Gainey is an unpretentious woman who lives every day intentionally. She didn't always live that way. A few years back, Gainey was a struggling young wife and, as she called herself, a "boy mom." She was exhausted every single day.

She says, "I was not prepared for the mental and physical strength needed to mother two little boys, the youngest of which was only five months old at the time. I was anxious all the time and had no joy and peace." In fact, Gainey did not have the spiritual, emotional, and physical energy to be the wife, mother, daughter, or any other role she had envisioned for herself.

She struggled to find a better way, and needed to start with something familiar to her. She had been a competitive athlete in college, so she understood the discipline required to take control of her health. So, she began by committing to exercise daily. That one decisive action launched a groundswell of changes in her life.

As she saw changes in her body and mental attitude, Gainey became more intentional in other aspects of her life. Now, she starts her day with the Lord before the family rises. She says, "Beginning my day intentionally with prayer sets a fertile ground for the remainder of my day."

Living intentionally in spirit and health has become Gainey's work, too. She runs an online health-and-fitness business, where she helps others achieve this same mindfulness. It's interesting to hear of her business growth and how she manages it intentionally, as well. For example, although fifty to one hundred clients contact her daily, she is intentionally unavailable at certain times and trains her team to do the same. She takes care of client needs, but carefully stages when and how she does that each day.

During the writing of this book, Gainey gave birth to a baby girl. She is no longer just a "boy mom!" She says she is still tired, but is no longer depleted at the end of the day. She has transformed her life to one full of joy, peace, contentment, and good health.

Just as Jami Gainey is more disciplined and has learned to let intentionality stream throughout her life, so can you. Like her, you can make a decision to start somewhere. It doesn't have to be some huge, monumental thing. Choose one thing to do purposefully, make a plan of execution, track your progress, and go from there.

Add to the plan tomorrow. Understand that the plan won't turn out exactly as you conceived it, but keep moving forward. Another of Gainey's principles could be a game changer for you: "Learn to ride through growing pains and periods of messiness in life." Nothing in life comes in a straight line or neatly packaged boxes. Strive to accept the untidiness of living and be at peace as things change.

I love Gainey's story because it demonstrates how powerful intention is for improving your life. Intentionality—the act of being deliberate or purposeful—is truly her legacy, because she lives it and then teaches others to replicate it in their lives.

Your legacy may be different from hers, but you can use the same deliberateness to build your legacy. She proves that you don't need a long list of changes to get started on your legacy. Just decide on one thing that you want to bequeath on your job or in the community, and start doing it right now—with *intention*.

You may think you don't have time, but you do. It's a matter of making it a priority. You have the same amount of time that everyone else has. Look at where you waste your time, and decide to reallocate that time to focus on building an intentional legacy.

Legacy Begins at Any Age

I'm sure you've heard old adages on age, like "Age is but a number," "Age is no guarantee of maturity," "Age is of no importance unless you are a cheese." Olympic track-and-field gold medalist Jackie Joyner-Kersee said one of my favorite quotes on age: "Age is no barrier. It's a limitation you put on your mind."

There is no age or right time to begin creating your legacy. In fact, now is the best time, regardless of your age and your status in life. Now is the time to get on with it. You have a limited amount of time on this earth, so get on with leaving that legacy now.

There are people of all ages who are living their legacy. Their stories are so encouraging.

Marley Dias is an avid reader. She was probably not thinking of a legacy when she launched #1000BlackGirlBooks in November 2015. Her initiative to find books featuring black girls as main characters shouldn't have been groundbreaking, but it was. At age ten, Dias set a goal to collect one thousand books and donate them to children. Her campaign brought to light the lack of diversity in children's literature.

In three years, Dias exceeded her goal, donating more than eleven thousand books to black girls. Her efforts thrust her into the national spotlight, even landing her a featured spot on Forbes' 30 Under 30 list in 2018. At just thirteen years old, she is a force to be reckoned with. She has already begun a legacy built on insightful activism, and she encourages other young people to find their passion and get active with it.

Dias's new mission is to encourage racial harmony. She is operating within her purpose of being of service to others. She clearly understands the power of being intentional.

For some, being intentional evolves as a result of a tragic incident. When Ernestine Shepherd and her sister embarked on a fitness routine, Shepherd was fifty-six years old, what for many is considered on the other end of the age spectrum. Shepherd's sister died suddenly, leaving her devastated. She was so traumatized that she lost her desire to go to the gym. A few months into mourning her sister's death, a friend mentioned that the sister would want Shepherd to continue what they had started. Shepherd agreed and renewed her commitment to working out.

Now, at age eighty-four (at the time of this writing), Shepherd has transformed her body and her life. In 2010, at age seventy-five, she was recognized by the *Guinness Book of World Records* as the oldest female competitive bodybuilder in the world. Traveling the world as a speaker and bodybuilder, she encourages other mature men and women to get fit. She says she has never been happier or more fulfilled in her life. This is what she was born to do.

Ernestine Shepherd was very intentional in defining her future. She is certainly building a legacy for all to see. She is an excellent example of what you can become with specific goals, discipline, and perseverance, regardless of age.

Ronald Wilson Reagan is best known as the fortieth president of the United States. There is much debate about his legacy as it relates to his long-term impact on the United States economy; however, most will agree that he brought a peaceful end to the Cold War, restored American confidence in its leadership, and increased American pride. Aside from his political legacy, Reagan established a legacy of commitment to serving others very early in his life.

Reagan, known as Dutch back in 1926, was fifteen years old when he became a lifeguard in Lowell Park near his home in Dixon, Illinois. He worked there diligently every summer for seven years. During that time, Reagan saved seventy-seven people from drowning. He kept a record of each save by making a notch on a wooden log. He was doing his job, but this was the beginning of Reagan's legacy of commitment to serving others. Later, in presidential speeches, he often reminded the American people of his core values of faith, family, community, peace, and freedom.

There are thousands of stories of ordinary and famous people like these who were inspired to make a difference and create a legacy that lasts. You probably know some personally. Who are the people in your circle whose legacy you can recount? What are they doing that inspires you to create a legacy of your own? What family member legacy can you adopt as your own?

BE DELIBERATE: PLAN YOUR LEGACY

Never fear to deliberately walk through dark places, for that is how you reach the light on the other side.
—Vernon Howard

You might consider it pretentious to plan a legacy, but what you leave behind can—and should—be premeditated. Remember, you leave a legacy, even if not deliberately. Be in control of yours. Envision what you want others to take away from the way you lead your life.

Consider individual groups of people in your life. What do you want to leave your company or coworkers when you move on to another opportunity? What do you want your siblings to gain from observing your life? What will you leave your children that will appear in the lives of your grandchildren?

You should care about what you leave in people, the legacy that will endure as you move through your life. You want it to make you proud—not with arrogance, but with gratification.

Here is a great example of why you should care. It may seem a bit over the top, but it nails the point.

About a hundred years ago, a French newspaper confused a man and his brother, and wrongly printed which one had died. The living brother was horrified to see his name in the obituary column. Once he regained his composure, his second thought was to find out what people had said about him. Headlines and the obituary purportedly read, "The Dynamite King dies and the Merchant of Death is dead." Both were referring to an explosion that occurred in his laboratory killing five people, including one of his brothers.

The man was Alfred Nobel. He was indeed the proud inventor of dynamite, but didn't like being called a merchant of death. He asked himself, *Is this how I am going to be remembered?* He brooded over this moniker and decided that it was not the legacy he wanted to leave.

From that day on, Nobel started working earnestly toward peace. He established the international Nobel Prize awards, and endowed the institution with most of his wealth when he died. Nobel's work to invent dynamite is still important, but he is most remembered today for creating the coveted Nobel Prize.

Just as Alfred Nobel redefined his values, you should step back and do the same. If, like Nobel, you don't like the legacy you might leave when you depart a place, you can change it—right now.

I'm reminded of the movie *It's a Wonderful Life*. You don't have the gift of seeing what others think and love about you once you are gone, as the character George Bailey did; however, you can choose one thing that you want them to remember and build it before you leave this earth. So, where do you begin?

You use your *why* to springboard into your legacy intentionally. Start with your desired end result and work backward. Your legacy can be as simple or as grand as you can imagine, and it can reach into one or many aspects of your life.

One of my employees, I'll call her Anne, was really good at her job. So good, in fact, that no one else could perform the job. This was in part because she had incorporated functions that weren't exactly in her job description. Our department had come to depend on her to perform those functions well for the good of the team. Anne was determined to be indispensable and wanted no part of teaching anyone else how she did what she did. This was a problem for me.

What if something happened to Anne and she couldn't come to work? What if she had to take leave to care for a sick family member? We would have been in trouble. I explained to Anne how horrible this was for the team and for her, too. I reassured her of how valuable she was, and assured her that she could do even more if she paved the way for someone to follow her. With encouragement and support, Anne created a comprehensive desk guide, which was eventually used by several of Anne's successors. With more insight into all the skills Anne possessed, I created a new job for her that allowed her to use her strengths and to build on them.

In addition to those you impact at work, there are others in your circle of influence whom you want to be impacted by your legacy. What do you want your children and grandchildren to take away from how you live? You may demonstrate unbelievable courage in difficult life circumstances, and want your family to know your story and aspire to live accordingly.

The same with friendship. You may have an incredible gift of camaraderie, building a number of close relationships that last for decades. Perhaps others in your present circle of influence, as well as your future generations, will marvel at your generosity to others. These are often unsung virtues, but may be just the ones you want your grandchildren to appreciate about you.

You already know that your legacy impacts others now and into the future. Those future generations might be your friends, your coworkers, your extended relatives, and of course, your direct descendants, among others.

Imagine that the year is 2118, and a descendant is checking out your family tree. Finding ancestors and the genesis of families will undoubtedly become easier as digital and scientific tools progress. Your descendant will see where you fit on the tree and how they are related to you. They click on your name, and details about you pop up. Aside from your vocation and hobbies, what do you want them to learn about how you lived your life? What characteristics about you will they discover? What evidence of these characteristics will you leave as clues? Which of your behaviors or actions do you want them to adopt as their own? What stories will they read that indicate the legacy you created?

As for me, I want my grandchildren and great-grandchildren to mirror my compassion for others and my thirst for learning. Additionally, I want them to see how I persevered through personal hardships while maintaining—and even growing in—faith and joy. No one is guaranteed a life of ease. I can speak from personal experience that life can be exceptionally hard, but you can live every day with gratitude, contentment, and joy. When telling stories and sharing pictures about me, I want them to see joy in my face, in spite of the painful challenges I have faced.

Lastly, I want them to remember to pass on specific family tenets. I absolutely love hearing my daughter tell my granddaughter the same guideposts that my mother and grandmother shared with me.

Your One Thing

If you could give one thing to the world—or to your small corner of the world (your community)—what would it be? If you're a big thinker, like a gentleman in my community, you might think on a global scale. He is the founder of a nonprofit called The Last Well, a charity that provides access to clean water to the entire nation of Liberia. Now, that's a *huge* one-thing challenge. The nonprofit intends to drill wells in every Liberian community by 2020. It is well (pardon the pun) on its way to impacting an entire country and leaving a legacy that counts for so many in need.

Your one thing could be more localized. Perhaps you want to impact the school that's around the corner from your home by volunteering to read to children after school. Are you naturally a good organizer? You could see to it that every child in your neighborhood has a safe place to play after school. Work with the businesses and other like-minded community activists to turn an old space into a nice place for children, perhaps even calling it the "Legacy House." It could be a lasting space for adults to learn to read or gain a new skill.

By using your gifts and your *why,* you can create something lasting. So, what is your one thing?

Perhaps yours is (or will be) a legacy of creation. What have you always wanted to create, but haven't? Identify small and big things that you really want to create for yourself or others. You are blessed to be an innately creative being. Your creativity can take so many forms. Creativity can be inspirational, emotional, or cognitive.

Perhaps you want to decorate a space, establish a garden, create new software, paint a mural or a house, write a book of poetry, carve a piece of wood, bake a delicious cake, open an online store, sew clothes or accessories, or develop new modes of transportation. There is a mound of research that proves the positive impact of creative endeavors on our brains, bodies, and society.

So, whatever your creative bent, start moving on it now. Make time in your week to focus on bringing your creation to fruition. Tell someone what you're up to. You'll want to make progress that you can share with your friends and family when they ask how it's going.

I experienced this firsthand when I embarked on writing this book. The minute I started screaming to the world that I was writing, I had to truly buckle down and get it done. Although I was disciplined and eager to write, family and social-media friends helped hold me accountable for maintaining my writing schedule. Your circle of influence will do the same for you. Tell them of your intention to draw on your creative talents in forming your legacy.

Regardless of your age, now is the time to think about and plan the legacy you will leave professionally and personally. Your world view may be big or small, and that's okay. Focus on the people and situations you want to impact most.

You Gotta Own It

When I was a teenager, my mother was my greatest inspiration and supporter. While encouraging me, she frequently admonished that if I wanted to succeed in this life, then it was up to me to make it happen. "It's up to you. You own your success," she would say.

Many years later, I learned of the simple quote by William H. Johnsen: "If it is to be, it is up to me." Whether my mother or Johnsen actually created the sentiment isn't of concern to me. What matters is that these simple words have driven me to take responsibility for all of my actions, particularly with regard to leaving a legacy that counts.

My mother also warned about having the best intentions, but a lazy butt. She would quote the aphorism "The road to hell is paved with good intentions." All of this meant that there is action required to reach your goals. You have to set your goals and do the work. Some people covet the achievements of others, but are not willing to do the work to get similar results. They want the accolades or the good feeling of having done something positive, but they don't want to put in the work that's required. Hence, they have good intentions and lazy butts.

When you don't take responsibility for realizing your potential, you can become your own worst enemy. Doubt speaks to you more often than you'd like. You may not recognize how quietly it sneaks into your thoughts and vocabulary. The words "maybe," "can't," and "later" become a common part of your lexicon, and you lose the desire and the passion for legacy building.

When life seems hard, you think you can't create a legacy, because you don't have the right kind of background, your parents weren't muckety-mucks, or you went to the wrong college (or didn't attend one at all). You're in a comfort zone, and fear you may lose what you have if you step out into something new. None of these things matter. You are born with the potential to do something fabulous in your life. You have been given gifts and talents. You've either honed or can hone skills to take you where you want to be. It's really up to you. You've got to own it.

Every pot must sit on its own bottom.
—Grandma Rosa Lee Green Spann

My grandmother Rosa was born in 1908 during some hard times for black people, especially for a black woman. She had little "book learning," as she called it, but the words of God were emblazoned on her heart and mind. Her life's experiences and God's words gave her great wisdom to share. She had a wise saying for just about everything.

One of my favorites of her many sayings that she'd share with us, seemingly out of the blue, was "Every pot must sit on its own bottom." That used to drive me crazy when I was little. I thought, *Well, of course the pot sits on its bottom. Otherwise, how can it be used?* In my infinite six-year-old wisdom, Grandma seemed a little slow if she thought she was telling me something useful. It took me a little while to connect the dots on that saying. When I finally did, I adopted it as my own. Every pot must sit on its own bottom to navigate through life successfully.

You have to own your life—the good and the bad. Every decision, act, and spoken word is yours to take responsibility for. If you don't like something about your life, it's up to you to change it. If you don't like your job, find one that better suits you, or determine how to make the one you have more impactful for you and your employer. Then, explain to your supervisor why the job needs to be changed for the good of customers, employees, or other relevant stakeholders. Don't complain about what you don't like. Be responsible for creating what you want.

The law of the universe has proven that you attract what you put out in the world. If you want more love in your life, you have to give more love. If you want people to be more understanding of you, then you have to be more tolerant and understanding of the next person. You get more when you give more.

There is a small catch, however. Be prepared to receive the love, kindness, understanding, etc. that comes your way, even if it's not exactly in the form that your heart desires. It's like when you pray for something, but don't recognize God's response because it isn't exactly what you expected.

For example, a good friend of mine had been praying for a companionable mate. She prayed that God would send her a man who was kind, humorous, spiritual, enjoyed exploring new places and experiences, and was business-minded. God answered her prayers. He sent her a man who had all the qualities she desired. The man is playful and makes her laugh wildly until her tummy hurts. He is extremely kind and thoughtful in ways that speak to her heart. He understands her ambition and supports her commitment to her business pursuits. My friend appreciates these and many other of his attributes; however, he didn't come in the package that she had envisioned. He is extremely tall, so he stands over just about everyone around. She doesn't personally like garnering that much attention. He has a big, round belly, and not the taut body she prefers. He is inquisitive and humorous, but just a little too loud.

My advice to her was to first be thankful. Be glad that God heard and answered her prayers (and in fairly short order). Then, examine what the man offers and what she needs. The jury is still out on her decision, but I believe she will keep him, even though he isn't exactly what she expected.

The life you want will not likely come in a neatly wrapped bundle, either. Just as God answered my friend's prayers, He will guide you in creating your legacy, but you have to choose to follow directions. In the end, it is up to you to do the work necessary to create a life full of meaning.

SHARE YOUR GIFTS
AND TALENTS FOR GOOD

It is a blessing to have your own unique talents. "We have different gifts, according to the grace given to each of us" (Romans 12:6). No two people have the exact same gift. You and your sister may both be gifted with musical talent, but the expression of those gifts is likely different.

Almost all faiths instruct you to pay homage to the giver of your gifts, and that the gifts are not given for you to hoard and enjoy solely for yourself. They are to be used for the good of the whole, whether that whole is your family, local community, or the world community. This is a universal philosophy. The belief that you are here for a purpose is what makes life meaningful. Additionally, the belief that you are to commune and work with others for the common good can be found from the beginning of time.

A hundred times a day I remind myself that my life
depends on the labors of other men, living and dead,
and that I must exert myself in order to give in the
measure as I have received and am still receiving.
—Albert Einstein

You are part of a bigger society in which all members are mutually dependent on one another. The talents and gifts you possess are needed for the whole society or community. Be clear what yours are so you can use and share them appropriately. Using your talents and gifts where needed is called stewardship. You are the steward, or custodian, of the gifts until they are needed to serve others. "For just as each of us has one body with many members, and these members do not all have the same function, so in Christ we, though many, form one body, and each member belongs to all the others" (Romans 12:4).

You can't always measure the joy you give others when you share your talents, even on the smallest level. But, you can relish in the enormous satisfaction you get when you do.

My mother-in-law, Susan Hilliard Hudson, spent her career as a schoolteacher and guidance counselor, where she constantly poured her love and knowledge into the lives of children; however, her enduring optimism and love of writing is where she really gave to others. She wrote letters of encouragement, affirmation, and gratitude every day for decades. If you had the pleasure of meeting her, she would have asked for your address, and within a few days you would have received a lovely handwritten letter from her. She wrote strangers, incarcerated men and women, family, and friends.

She made you feel like you were the most awesome person in the world. Her letters of gratitude for every little thing you did for her or for someone close to her were just as powerful. They were reminders that small acts of kindness are to be given and treasured. She demonstrated that serving others creates lasting fulfillment. Serving others blesses your soul and heart like nothing else, whether you are the giver or the receiver of the gifts.

If your dream is only about you, it's too small.
— Ava DuVernay

Regardless of what you're great at doing, seek opportunities to give it away to make a positive impact on others. In this way, you are leaving your legacy that counts.

I am on the board of a charity that I can't give enough to these days. The Dallas, Texas,–based nonprofit empowers women by helping them develop financial stability, learn new skills, become better parents, and build their own businesses. It's a place where people start new chapters, new adventures, new habits, and even new families. The organization would not be successful without its large cadre of volunteers, who teach women how to become great mothers, to manage their finances, to develop business plans, and to open businesses.

Volunteers are needed everywhere. Organizations appreciate whatever amount of time you can give them. As my mother would say, "Give little or much—it all adds up over time."

The key points I want you to take away from this chapter are simple:

- You are the custodian of the skills, aptitude, and talents you need to accomplish your assignment on this earth. Own them, use them, and hone them to magnify your impact on your life and that of others.

- Intentions are good only when acted upon. You already know, or are in the process of discerning, your purpose. Make it a priority, for knowing your purpose is of great importance. Once you are certain of that, you can size up how to best use your talents intentionally in every aspect of your life.

- Treat intentionality as a mandate—a directive to create a plan for realizing your potential. It's a requisite for leading a preeminent life. Why drift along when you can carve out a studied path for making a difference? Start now. Be purposeful and deliberate in creating your legacy.

- Remember, every pot must sit on its own bottom. You own everything about you: your attitude, your fitness, your decisions, your actions, your happiness, and your contentment. It is really freeing to own and accept accountability for your actions and decisions. When you mess up—and you will—take stock of what went wrong, and determine how to improve future actions and decisions that you make. Sometimes it is only in your rearview mirror that you can see opportunities to do and be better.

In the end, what you undertake can have immeasurable impact on others now and maybe in the future. Be as accountable for that impact as you are to yourself. And lastly, take pleasure in the role you play on life's stage.

Legacy Leaps

For ideas to live more deliberately as you create your legacy, download the following resources at www.TerrieHudson.com/legacyleaps:

- Intentional Living Assessment Worksheet
- Checklist of Thirty Things to Do Intentionally

CHAPTER FIVE

HOW TO DISCOVER YOUR LEGACY

*Those who have a "why" to live
can bear with almost any "how."*
—Viktor E. Frankl, Holocaust Survivor

One of my favorite places to hang out when I was a little girl was in the back room of my Grandma Rosa's house. The room was located right off the kitchen, so it was warm and cozy. My grandma would sit in the big rocking chair crocheting something for one of us, while I dangled my feet over the side of the bed. One rainy afternoon, we were in there listening to rain pummel the tin roof when, out of the blue, I asked, "Grandma, what happens to us when we die?"

She told me that our bodies die, but our spirits go to be with the Lord. I asked lots of other questions about this process, and two questions in particular stick in my mind. First, "How will I know your spirit when I get to Heaven?"

She thought about this for a while and answered, "You will know me because our spirits will recognize each other. You are my blood. I will know you."

Grandma Rosa's answer to my second question was really profound. I asked, "What is our purpose on Earth if all we do is die in the end?"

She didn't hesitate on this one. She told me that God has given each of us an assignment. Of course,

I wanted to know what mine was and when I was going to get it. I remember her smiling as she continued crocheting and telling me that I had to figure it out with God's help.

It took me years to know for sure, but Grandma Rosa was correct. It takes work to determine your purpose, and it takes intention to establish a legacy that counts.

Scientists conduct systematic research, and analyze loads of data to explain or predict everything that happens in the universe. But, there is no science for how to create your legacy. Even the interdisciplinary fields of social sciences have no answer for you on this. You have to figure it out. As you do, you must trust that God has already placed within you the ability, the passion, and the intellect to create your lasting legacy.

The highly acclaimed astrophysicist Neil deGrasse Tyson made an interesting statement when recalling how his interest in astronomy began. He was nine years old when he first visited the Hayden Planetarium. He has said many times, "So strong was the imprint (of the night sky) that I'm certain that I had no choice in the matter; that in fact, the universe called me." Tyson became so obsessed with the universe that by age eleven he decided to become an astrophysicist. He began fulfilling his purpose to become a space advocate and teach others about the universe. Today, Tyson heads the famed Hayden Planetarium, where he first laid eyes on the cosmos.

A lightning bolt of awareness may not hit your head or heart, as received by Neil deGrasse Tyson. You may not yet have a burning desire to do any one thing. Nonetheless, you can conceive one. Self-awareness is key to discovering your legacy. It takes internal reflection and introspection to fully learn what you're here to do. Some people use meditation to clear their minds while pursuing the meaning of life. Others find that a more direct approach, similar to the one described next, works for them. You will have to assess what feels right to you.

I recommend a reflective approach to begin creating your legacy. Although it is contemplative, you need not follow or use meditation techniques. The tools you need are simple:

- **Time**. You don't want to rush this process, so expect to work on yourself over the course of a few weeks. Block out thirty to sixty minutes per day on your calendar. You may need less or more time to realize your goals, but start with two weeks. If it takes you a month or more, just keep going. This time is for you to listen and connect to your purpose.

- **Space.** Select a space in your home or wherever you find peace and quiet. If your house is a boisterous one, you may have to create a tranquil space in your garage or outside in a corner of your backyard.

Wherever you choose is fine as long as it is fairly silent, and you can be comfortable, relaxed, and uninterrupted.

- **Notebook.** Select a journal that you will use only for this process. You will capture your thoughts, doodles, and anything else pertinent as you follow the process outlined below. Journals are personal by their very nature. Some people find it soothing to write in one that fits their personality (e.g. businesslike or floral, colorful, or effervescent). Choose one that feels good in your hands and is easy to write in.

Now you are ready to begin your self-examination. Introspection isn't really taught anywhere on a broad scale, so you may need practice to get the hang of it. Looking deep inside yourself isn't always easy. In fact, your mind will wander or focus on everything that you perceive to be "wrong" with you. When you begin this journey, put aside all negative thoughts. Don't focus on the distractions that pull you away from this effort. You should be in your quiet space, where you can control your thinking without interruption.

Take a few deep breaths to center yourself and hush your mind. Focus on you. Use the following questions to begin gathering information to build your *why.* Record your answers in your journal.

Assess what brings your heart true joy. You play numerous roles every day. You are employee, employer, spouse, teacher, parent, sibling, and friend. What brings you great pleasure in each of the roles you play? When do you feel the most joy in these roles? What are you doing at those moments? How do you express that joy? Be thoughtful and specific about the answers. Write down everything that comes to your mind without judgment.

Explore your environment. It's easy to take your work and play environments for granted. How often have you reflected on where you are at your happiest? Probably not often, if ever. Now is the time to do it. Where are you when you have your most joyous feelings? Is it a particular type of building? Is it the garden you pass on the way to work? Are you joyous every time you cross the bridge from the city to a more rural setting, or vice versa? What elements of your work space uplift you? Is it the light that pours in through the windows near your desk?

Be specific about the spaces that enrich your life. Perhaps you are enlivened whenever you're around water or beautiful skies. What color are the spaces where you feel best? What part of the world or your country excites you? Consider the places you have visited in the world. Are there some that stir up memories that you would like to experience on a regular basis by living there or visiting more often? If you don't travel enough to answer this question, what countries have you read about? What intrigues you about them? The US State Department estimates that only 9 million Americans live outside of the US. Maybe you want to become an expat.

Identify the people who bring you joy. This can be a curious exploration for you. Think hard about those who make you feel happy or content every time you meet them, and those who you naturally want to serve or to whom you always want to give. Is it a single individual or a group of people? Are they children or adults? What age group are they? What are they doing that separates them from others in your life? How do these people interact with you? Do they challenge you or let you be? It is helpful to flip your mind around and determine which people interactions you dislike.

Assess your natural talents, gifts, and skills. Write down the things that come effortlessly to you. Like everyone, you have specific gifts and talents that allow you to perform some tasks and jobs more easily than others do. I enjoy speaking to large groups. I can't remember a time when that didn't come easily to me. I am gifted with words, voice tone, and an ability to genuinely connect with people. I use them all when speaking. And just so you know, that doesn't mean I don't get nervous. But, once I get on stage, I use those nerves to energize me and do what I love.

Some people are naturally good with numbers. Some have a penchant for describing complex concepts in a way that others can easily understand. Maybe you lean toward more left-brain-dominant skills, such as foreign languages, the written or spoken word, or music. Some people are really good at spatial things; they can see what others can't see. Perhaps drawing is easy for you. Remember, your skills and talents aren't just for you. So, if you are a gifted artist, use that gift so others can enjoy it.

If you are having difficulty identifying anything meaningful in some areas, you may need to think from opposite experiences. In that case, identify the functions you know, without a doubt, that you do not enjoy. These can be things that you abhor and are unwilling to do.

As an example, some jobs include tasks that require you to perform the same motions day in and day out. The thought of doing the same repetitive motion over and over every day might make your head hurt. Write down those things that bring you distress.

Perhaps you prefer working alone, or you like solitary avocations. If so, think of what you don't like about working and playing with others. There should be no judgment in your thinking, only clarity and honesty.

This is not the time to ask for feedback from anyone. No opinions except your own matter here. Just be sure you have been honest with your answers. This is all about you and what shapes you.

LEGACY LEAPS

PUTTING IT ALL TOGETHER

You have a lot of information about yourself now covering who, what, where, and when you are authentically you. Now that you know what truly brings you joy, the environments that awaken your senses, your emotions around specific types of people, and what you don't want to do, you have the fodder to discover your legacy.

Contemplate the information carefully and with an open mind. Do not underestimate the value of regularly sitting in silence as this process unfolds. Silence allows you to hear and receive what you need to know. When your thoughts wander, jot down what comes to you, and then bring your thoughts back to the task at hand.

This part of the process should take some time. Don't rush while working through this. Drill down if your initial answers are too vague to offer valuable insights. Notice that all the elements that you captured have an underlying theme or common threads running through them. Group them now, if you can.

You may experience a variety of emotions as you review what you've written. This is all good. Highlight the things that quicken in your spirit. Keep working until you feel you have clarity.

Then, synthesize your outcome to capture the what, who, and where you will most comfortably start leveraging your *why*. Organize the information into this framework:

- I am most happy working with

  _____

  (Describe people/animals/plants).

- I prefer being

  _____

  (Describe the environment).

- I am most gifted in

  _____

  (One or two areas only).

- I feel in my soul that my legacy is to

  _____

  _____

  _____

  (State your legacy in the most simple single statement you can).

- I will intentionally demonstrate my legacy by

  _____

  (State how you will begin living out your legacy).

You have just identified what truly sculpts you. It's feasible that you still have more work to do to know who you are. That's okay. Continue to do the work.

You are the author and illustrator of your life. If you want to truly lead a life full of meaning and boundless fulfillment, invest time to discover your legacy. Make it a priority right now. Be sure to conduct your personal assessment without input from others. Forget about opinions, should they be offered, regarding your self-discoveries. You are only interested in determining what/who brings you great joy and the environments that inspire you to feel that way.

Searching for and finding your legacy is the greatest gift you will ever give yourself. When you're wholly connected to your purpose, you will shape and experience the future differently. Your life will be altogether richer, fuller, and forever changed. In addition, you will change the beings that you encounter as you walk in your legacy.

You've done the work. Now, put it to use.

CHAPTER SIX

YOUR
LEGACY COUNTS

Your life's journey isn't just for you. Find your why,
and get busy leaving nuggets for others.
—Terrie Davoll Hudson

Life is short, no matter how many years you are blessed to live. Make yours count with a lasting impact on your family, friends, and the community at large. I began this book sharing stories about my mother and grandparents. The last story here is about my mother's enduring desire to keep learning and inspire others until the day she left this earth.

Mu was determined to leave the factory where she made shirtwaist dresses. She wanted to earn a bachelor's degree. She worked during the day, went to school at night, and graduated with honors, all while managing a household comprised of my dad and three young children. We were still young when she fulfilled her calling and became a brilliant high school teacher. She loved teaching and reaching into the very souls of her students. She didn't stop there. She went on to earn a master's in education administration by taking classes at night and over the course of many summers.

Once she retired, Mu continued performing what she called "goodness and mercy outreach." She and my dad provided money, food, and school supplies for teachers and students in the area. One day, she called me, saying she was returning to school. She wanted to marry her interest in education and her undying love for God by studying religion.

So, she enrolled in an online program. It wasn't easy, either. She had to purchase a new computer, learn to use the latest software, and become familiar with search engines and online portals. I laughed a lot during that time, as I became her teacher and technical-support manager.

I can't tell you how swollen my heart and eyes were as my father, brother, and I watched my seventy-six-year-old mother walk across the stage graduating with a PhD in biblical studies. Never letting anything hold her back—not poverty, children, or illness—Mu lived a life worth emulating. She gave everything she had to her family, students, and community. She left us with a can-do spirit, a commitment to helping others, and a thirst for continuous learning. As her students said when she died, "Mrs. Davoll was the epitome of an educator. She was tough, but ignited our love for history and learning. She was a great inspiration to us all. Her legacy lives on in the hundreds who still talk about the most fabulous teacher we ever had."

I don't know how she knew, but my mother walked in her purpose from the time she was a little girl with her slate and chalk teaching neighborhood kids and adults to read and write, right until she took her last breath. My purpose is different from my mother's, but like her, I want to walk in mine until I take my last breath.

Making a difference for others and impacting their lives up close and personal are the motivating drivers for my legacy. I've helped numerous people examine the potential risks and benefits of following their dreams and watched them soar. I've enjoyed supporting others achieve their educational pursuits, in spite of where they started in life or the difficult circumstances they encountered. I treasure the stories and feedback people share about their accomplishments. I rejoice in seeing how strong, resilient, and magnificent each person is and can be when I ask, "Why not?", help them build life plans, and then pour out encouragement into them.

Years from now, I want others to remember the impact I had on their grandparents, their parents, and themselves. I want them to share stories about how the spunky little black lady inspired them to reach their full potential. That's a legacy that means something to me.

Each stage of life is the right one to begin crafting a legacy. You can—and should—create your legacy now. There is no need to wait until you have matured or reached a particular milestone in life. Whether you are ten, thirty, or sixty years old, now is the time. The sooner you begin, the more fruitful your legacy will be during your lifetime.

Start by examining the legacies that were left to you. What philosophical values, material, and biological heritage did you receive? What will you keep and pass on to others? With little control over the biological gifts you inherit, you are left with material and values inheritances. Determining which of these to add to your greatest legacy is paramount to getting on the right journey early in life.

The broader society places a huge value on material bequests. Although there is nothing wrong with a focus on making money and gaining other material possessions to leave your family, I want to remind you of two things: First, financial and material things come and go. You can gain and lose them in the blink of an eye. There are countless stories of celebrities making piles of money, spending it freely, or encountering circumstances that drain them down to nothing.

Second, if you have money and material possessions to pass on, you are probably proud of the efforts you put forth to gain them. Your beneficiaries may not appreciate the ingenuity, hard work, and execution you put into acquiring them. So, with nothing more, you will bequeath the money and goods for others to enjoy, but not your work ethic. In fact, material legacy, without a legacy of guiding principles or values, is not likely sustainable over time.

Lasting and unforgettable legacies are linked to your values. You create legacies that help you and others grow when guided by them. That is why understanding what's important to you—what you value—is so crucial to setting the foundation for legacy. This foundation leads to a deeper understanding of your *why*. You know now that legacies are best created from the depths of your *why* (your purpose). Determining yours now will give you a lifetime of contentment and joy. The sooner you begin discovering your *why*, the more you will contribute. You will undoubtedly create a number of legacies in a variety of areas of your life.

Humans are complex beings with characteristics framed by past experiences, consequences of previous actions, and responses to life's intricacies. All of that, plus what you know about your beliefs, values, and purpose, is your guide.

Let your values and your *why* lead you to create legacies like the Little Free Libraries, #1000BlackGirl-Books, community gardens, or playground restorations, for example. You have your own unique and matchless ideas for creating or leveraging your legacy. There is no one like you, so your legacy at work, at play, and in your community will be unlike anyone else's. Get on with it!

Envision yourself appraising your contributions with satisfaction. Give yourself permission to go big and bold in conceiving your legacy. Sure, obstacles may arise, but you can overcome them one by one. Obstacles are simply bumps along the way and opportunities to learn and grow. What's to stop you from being the person others highlight and put in books? You have what it takes to create and leave an awesome legacy—one that really counts and lasts!

I am counting on you to get started. The time is now. Tell somebody what your intentions are so your friends and colleagues can cheer you on. Hopefully, some family and associates will be inspired to begin their own legacy-building work.

I wish you a lifetime of legacy building, triumphant joy in the midst of difficult circumstances, and stories that others share about you for decades to come. May your legacies bring contentment deep in your soul. Let nothing hold you back. Be intentional, be deliberate, be accountable, and enjoy your legacy journey.

Deposit your best in people, not your bank account, to leave a legacy that counts.
—Terrie Davoll Hudson

Legacy Contributors

Joni Arison

I want my sons to tell their children that I was always there for them. I had a great family life. I was a positive #girlboss with a leadership role in a Fortune 10 company. I was humble, kind, and took a genuine interest in people. I want to share these values with them: "Do your best, give it your all, treat people as you want to be treated, love what you do, balance your life, and love one another."

Diane Chesley

My legacy will be about family—those we're born into and those we choose along the way. I have often told my boys, Audie and Andrew, that family is everything. Audie knows he is to look out for his younger brother, Andrew, and that they should always remain a unit against all odds. They also know to look out for their aunt, my oldest sister, and her granddaughter, because that's what family does.

Several childhood friends are considered "aunts" and "uncles" to my boys, and I know these people would be there for them if ever needed. Some sorority sisters, lifelong friends, former colleagues, and students are very much like my own flesh and blood and are very much part of my family. Family is the nucleus of my foundation. I am who I am today because of all my "family."

Alexis Dennard

I want my legacy to be that I raised a God-fearing child who lives his full potential and brings forth continued generations of Dennards. I want my grandchildren and great-grandchildren to understand and know all the things I instilled in Kamari that my parents instilled in me: grace, hard work, love, appreciation, fun, exposure, grit, can-do, confidence/belief in self. I want my legacy to be that I cared and gave my time and talents unselfishly in the service of causes and organizations I cared for via boards or as an advocate. I want to be remembered as someone who loved the Lord and tried to live an upright life with beautiful family and friends. I made people laugh, smile, experience this world, challenge you to think, use your influence for good, and just appreciate the goodness of life.

Jami Lee Gainey

I want to be remembered for pointing people well to my savior; that I lived a generous and grateful life with five values: gratitude, growth, grace, generosity, and grit.

Debby Feir

There are three areas in which I hope my legacy will live on:

1. I want my students to always think critically, ask lots of questions, challenge the status quo, and challenge authority with respect. Most importantly, I hope they learn the importance of sharing what they know with someone else.

2. All the kids in the neighborhood—some are grown now—know that they can talk to me about anything. I am an adult they can trust. I want them to feel that they can tell people how they feel. Also, to use their instincts to guide them.

3. Family means "I have your back always." My nieces know that they can call on me for anything and I'll be there, whether it's to celebrate a success or help them move across country. They can count on me to tell them when they're wrong (always with love), and that says to them and other loved ones that family has your back in all circumstances.

Lorraine Igwe Toliver

My legacy is surviving the unknown, living and thriving in the unknown. I married a Nigerian and moved to Nigeria during the early 1970s. I survived being in a foreign country, bearing children there, and even living through several coups. I am a survivor and want my children and grandchildren to know how to do the same. One word that encapsulates how I feel about this is "blessed."

Write yours here:

Notable
Legacy Leaders

Adkins, Adele Laurie Blue
b. 1988
British singer-songwriter

Angelou, Maya (Marguerite Johnson)
1928–2014
American writer, poet, activist

Arison, Joni (Joanne) Cavallero
b. 1964
American business executive

Bush, George H. W.
1924–2018
Forty-first American president

Davoll, Catherine Spann
1934–2012
American educator

Dennard, Alexis Penelton
b. 1972
American businesswoman

Dias, Marley
b. 2005
American activist

DuVernay, Ava
b. 1972
American film director, producer, screenwriter

Edison, Thomas Alva
1897–1931
American inventor, businessman

Einstein, Albert
1879–1955
German theoretical physicist

Emerson, Ralph Waldo
1803–1882
American essayist, poet

Feir, Deborah B.
b. 1946
American business professional, educator

Fosdick, Raymond B.
1883–1972
American philanthropist, lawyer

Frankl, Viktor Emil
1905–1997
Austrian neurologist, Holocaust survivor

Gainey, Jami Lynn
b. 1987
American small-business owner

Howard, Vernon
1918–1992
American spiritual teacher, philosopher

Hudson, Susan Hilliard
1928–2012
American educator, writer

Hurston, Zora Neale
1891–1960
American author, anthropologist

Kotb, Hoda
b. 1964
American broadcast journalist

Mandela, Nelson
1918–2013
South African antiapartheid revolutionary, political
leader

Montaigne, Michel de
1533–1592
French philosopher

Nobel, Alfred
1833–1896
Swedish inventor, philanthropist

Norton, Richie
b. 1980
American author, business advisor

Reagan, Ronald
1911–2004
Fortieth president of the United States

Ralston, Aron
b. 1975
American outdoorsman, motivational speaker

Rumi (Jalal ad-Din ar-Rumi)
1207–1273
Persian Poet

Shepherd, Ernestine
b. 1936
American, oldest female competitive bodybuilder

Spann, Robert
1900–1965
American minister, boilermaker

Spann, Rosa Lee (nee Green)
1908–(1991)
American military laundress

Toliver, Lorraine Igwe
b. 1941
American lawyer, teacher

Tutu, Desmond
b. 1931
South African theologian, antiapartheid activist

Tyson, Neil deGrasse
b. 1958
American astrophysicist

Endnotes

Chapter 1

1. Wiktionary.com, s.v. "Character" usage notes, accessed September 2018, https://en.wiktionary.org/wiki/character.
2. Vocabulary.com, s.v. "Happenstance", accessed October 2018, https://www.vocabulary.com/dictionary/happenstance.

Chapter 3

3. NPR, "You Can Prepare Yourself: A Conversation with Adele," All Things Considered, November 24, 2015.
4. Bruce Britt, "Musicians Who Grapple with Stage Fright," GRAMMY.com, February 26, 2019, https://www.grammy.com/grammys/news/adele-van-halen-among-musicians-who-battle-stage-fright.
5. John R. Montopoli, LMFT, LPCC, "Public Speaking and Fear of Brain Freezes,"

National Social Anxiety Center (blog), February 20, 2017.

6. https://nationalsocialanxietycenter.com/2017/02/20/public-speaking-and-fear-of-brain-freezes/.

7. "About Us," Post-It, https://www.post-it.com/3M/en_US/post-it/contact-us/about-us/.

About the Author

Terrie Davoll Hudson is an award-winning business leader, inspiring motivational speaker, and professional coach with over thirty years of leadership in sales and operational excellence. While working for AT&T, she received AT&T's Vision of Excellence Award and was inducted many times into AT&T's prestigious President's Club and Achiever's Club. She is also an alumna of Leadership Georgia.

Terrie has spent a lifetime leading, coaching, and mentoring others. She is a passionate community advocate, deeply committed to educating women and lifting women and families out of poverty. She serves on the board of directors of WiNGS Dallas and of the Possible Woman Foundation, Inc.

She believes in living boldly and from her heart. Terrie loves theater, art, music, gardening, and dancing every chance she gets.

Terrie leaves a legacy of values rooted in giving to others, educating women, and persevering through tough experiences. She lives in Dallas, Texas, with her husband, Elliott, and their dog, Maxie.

For more information about Terrie's workshops and seminars, or to order copies of her book, visit www.TerrieHudson.com.

Connect
with the Author

Join the Legacy Circle

For free legacy resources that complement this book, go to www.terriehudson.com/leagacyleaps.

Bring Terrie Hudson to Your Organization

Terrie is known for her dynamic speaking style. She gives audiences authentic leadership principles and inspires them to lead and live boldly. Audiences walk away with practical and actionable ideas.

To book Terrie for your next event (Tea with Terrie Live or other appearances), email your request to info@terriehudson.com.

Thank You for Reading

Thanks for buying *Leave a Legacy that Counts*!

I hope it takes you on an intentional journey to create legacies that really matter to you.

If you enjoyed reading the book, please take a moment to leave a review on Amazon and Goodreads.

I'd love to hear from you. Use #legacyleaps when sharing your thoughts and comments on www.terriehudsom.com and your social media.

Blessings to you!

Terrie Davoll Hudson